About Our Alphabets & Frames

The alphabets in this book can be stitched by themselves, or they can be combined with the stunning frames that are designed to border them. Be inspired by our photographs; then use them as a jumping point for your own creations.

Stitch monograms, names or messages, and take ordinary items from plain to uniquely personal. Stitch them on premade products like bookmarks, bibs and fingertip towels, or on even-weave fabrics such as Aida cloth or linen.

The Frames: pages 2 to 7
Each of our 12 frames is designed to fit one or more of the alphabet styles. Each charted frame specifies which alphabet it was designed to adorn.

The Alphabets: pages 7 to 14
There are eight alphabets; each is great for stitched monograms, names or words.

How to Stitch: pages 15 and 16
Look here for directions on working from charts and stitching on even-weave fabrics.

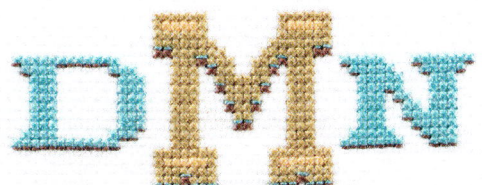

Using Weekend alphabet, outer initials on sample were stitched with #959 medium sea green; Backstitches were worked with #3858 medium rosewood. Using Country Casual alphabet, center initial on sample was stitched with #3827 pale golden brown, #3828 hazelnut brown and #3858 medium rosewood; backstitches were worked with #959 medium sea green.

Using Semiformal alphabet, outer initials on sample were stitched with #959 medium sea green. Using Super Size alphabet, center initial on sample was stitched with #702 kelly green, #959 medium sea green, #3811 very light turquoise and #3837 ultra dark lavender; backstitches were worked with #702 kelly green.

American School of Needlework • Berne, Indiana 46711 • DRGnetwork.com   Personalize It With Cross-Stitch • 1

Princess Frame

Design Size
36 wide x 38 high

CROSS-STITCH (2 strands)

DMC	ANCHOR	COLORS
333	119	Very dark blue violet
704	256	Bright chartreuse
894	27	Very light carnation
912	209	Light emerald green
3731	76	Very dark dusty rose

BACKSTITCH (2 strands)

DMC	ANCHOR	COLORS
333	119	Very dark blue violet
777	43	Very dark raspberry
373	176	Very dark dusty rose

ATTACH 3mm RHINESTONE

DARICE	COLOR
0683-T1AB	Crystal

 Letter placement

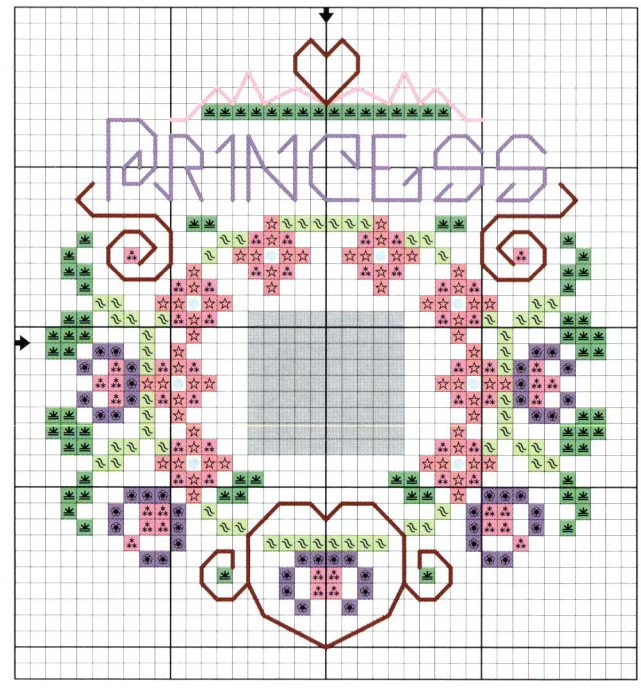

To personalize, use Junior Glamour Alphabet (page 13).
Model was stitched on antique white 14-count Aida fabric from Charles Craft, using DMC floss and crystal rhinestones from Darice. Initial on sample was stitched with #894 very light carnation. Stitched piece is shown mounted on a Keepsake Decor Memory Box from Crafty Productions Inc. and trimmed with a 4mm clear iridescent bead strand.

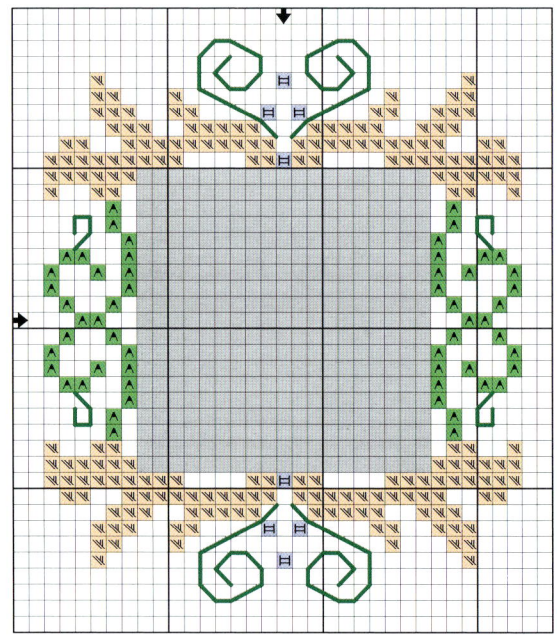

Vining Frame

Design Size
31 wide x 35 high

CROSS-STITCH (2 strands)

DMC	ANCHOR	COLORS
434	310	Light brown
904	258	Very dark parrot green
3842	164	Dark Wedgwood

BACKSTITCH (2 strands)

DMC	ANCHOR	COLOR
904	258	Very dark parrot green

Letter placement

To personalize, use Semiformal Alphabet (page 8).
Model was stitched on ivory 14-count Aida fabric using DMC floss. Initial on sample was stitched with #312 very dark baby blue. Stitched piece was inserted in an acrylic coaster, available from most needlecraft suppliers.

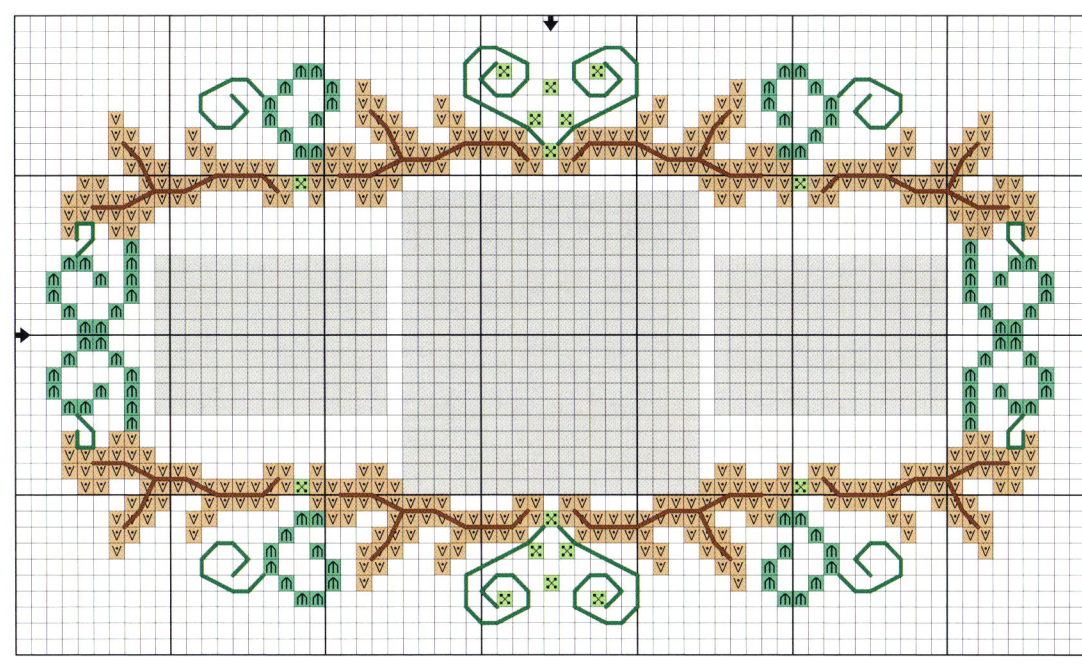

Vining Frame for 3-Letter Monogram

Design Size
65 wide x 36 high

CROSS-STITCH (2 strands)

DMC	ANCHOR	COLORS
701	227	Light green
907	255	Light parrot green
3826	1049	Golden brown

BACKSTITCH (2 strands)

DMC	ANCHOR	COLORS
701	227	Light green
938	381	Ultra dark coffee brown

☐ Letter placement

To personalize, use Weekend and Semiformal Alphabets (pages 7 and 8). Model was stitched on beige 14-count Aida fabric using DMC floss. Initials on sample were stitched with #3849 light teal green and #3847 dark teal green; backstitches were worked with #3847 dark teal green.

Flower Frame for Initial

Design Size
26 wide x 26 high

CROSS-STITCH (2 strands)

DMC	ANCHOR	COLORS
3803	972	Dark mauve
3832	28	Medium raspberry
3833	26	Light raspberry

☐ Letter placement

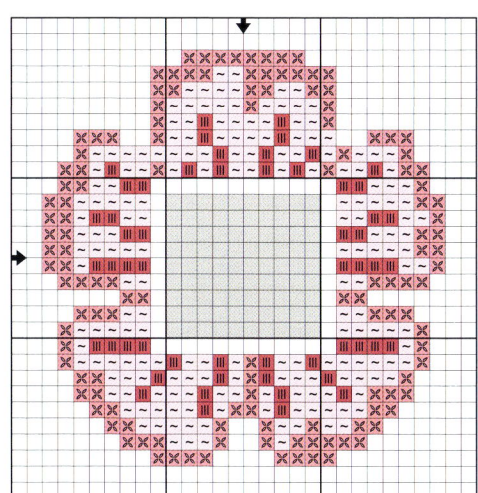

To personalize, use Junior Glamour Alphabet (page 13), leaving off rhinestones. Model was stitched with multiple motifs on ivory 18-count Aida fabric bookmark from Charles Craft using DMC floss. Name on sample was stitched with #3850 dark bright green.

American School of Needlework • Berne, Indiana 46711 • DRGnetwork.com

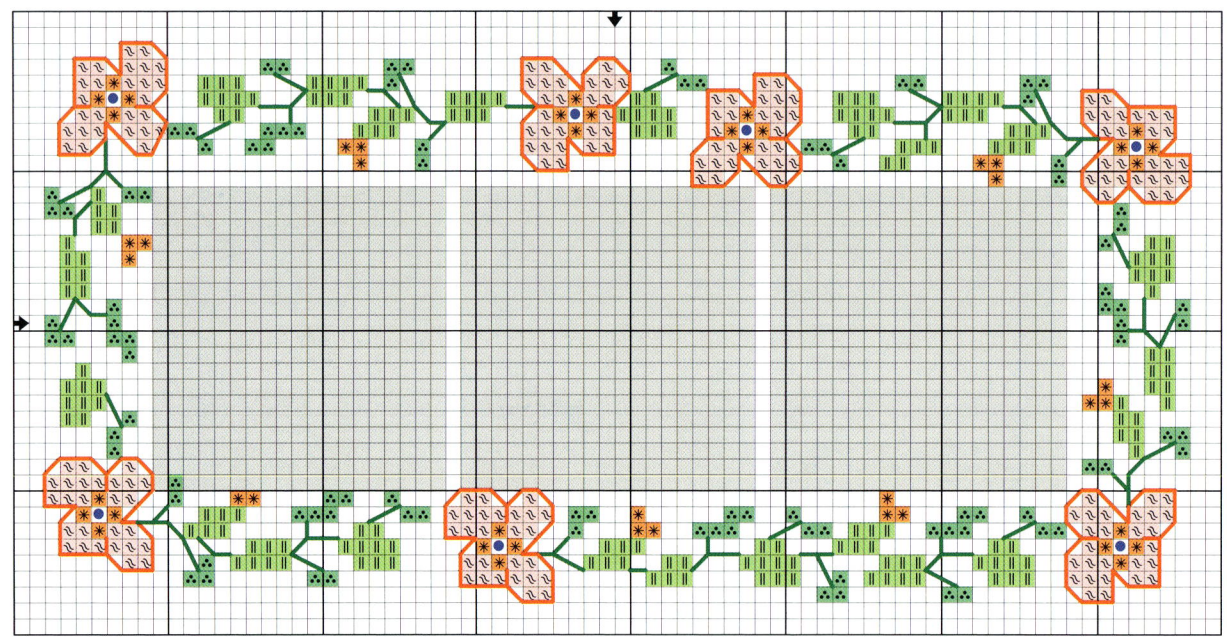

Blossom Frame

Design Size
74 wide x 35 high

CROSS-STITCH (3 strands)

DMC	ANCHOR	COLORS
352	9	Light coral
900	333	Dark burnt orange
907	255	Light parrot green
912	209	Light emerald green

BACKSTITCH (2 strands)

DMC	ANCHOR	COLORS
900	333	Dark burnt orange
912	209	Light emerald green

ATTACH BEAD

Pearlized pink seed bead

Letter placement

To personalize, use Semiformal Alphabet (page 8).
Model was stitched on white 11-count Aida fabric using DMC floss and pearlized seed beads. Initials on sample were stitched with #156 medium light blue violet.

Blossom Frame for One Initial

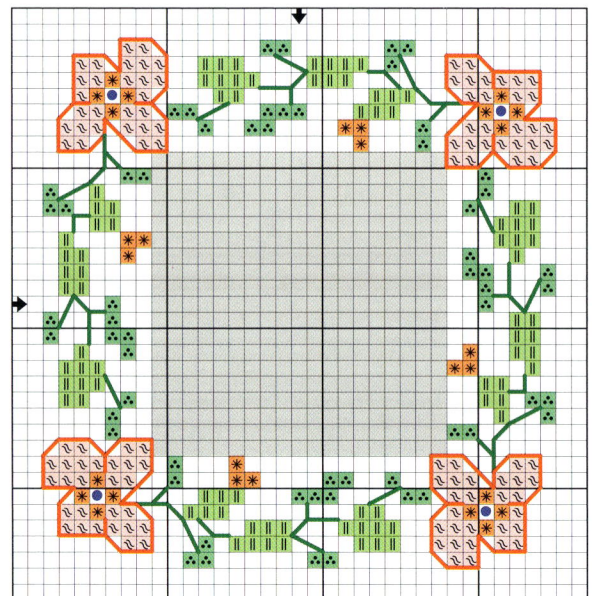

4 • Personalize It With Cross-Stitch American School of Needlework • Berne, Indiana 46711 • DRGnetwork.com

Butterfly Frame

Design Size
48 wide x 35 high
Design width will vary.

CROSS-STITCH (2 strands)

DMC	ANCHOR	COLORS
155	109	Medium dark blue violet
704	256	Bright chartreuse
894	27	Very light carnation
972	298	Deep canary
3846	1090	Light bright turquoise

BACKSTITCH (1 strand)

DMC	ANCHOR	COLORS
309	42	Dark rose
704	256	Bright chartreuse

Letter placement

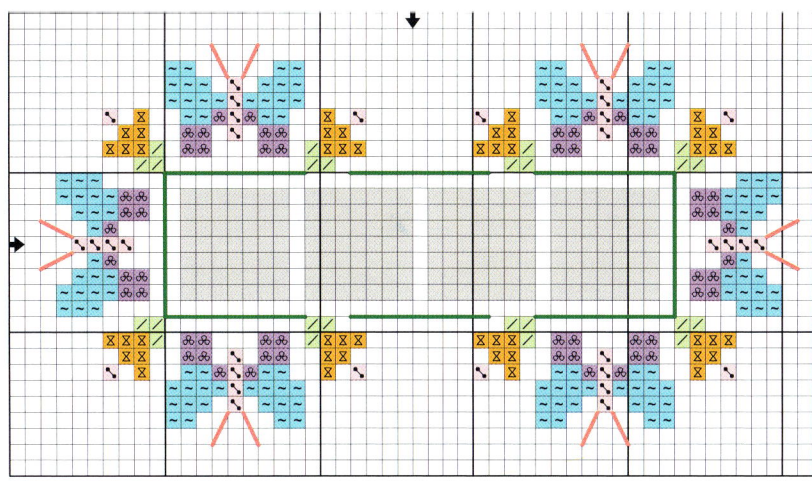

To personalize, use Petite Alphabet (page 11).
Model was stitched on ivory 14-count Aida fabric from Charles Craft using DMC floss. Stitch desired name, then stitch right and left borders around it. Extend or shorten center green lines as needed. Name on sample was stitched with #309 dark rose.

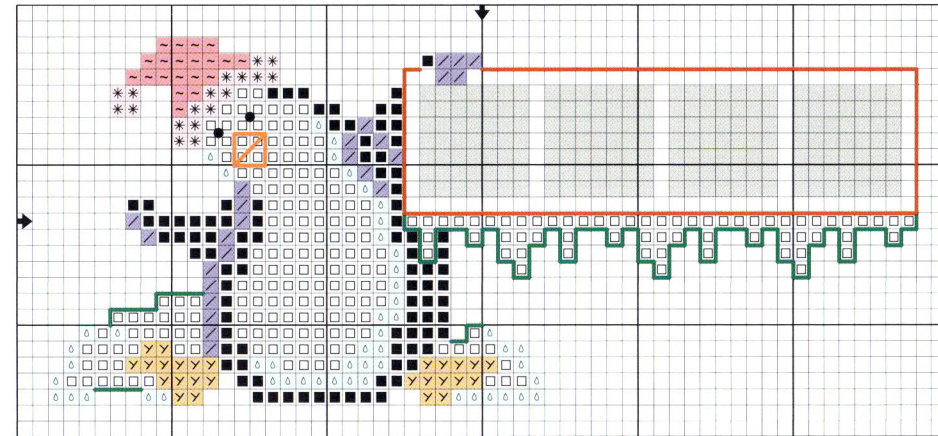

Penguin Frame

Design Size
56 wide x 23 high
Design width will vary.

CROSS-STITCH (2 strands)

DMC	ANCHOR	COLORS
Blanc	2	White
156	118	Medium light blue violet
310	403	Black
498	1005	Dark red
721	925	Medium orange spice
964	185	Light sea green
3801	1098	Very dark melon

BACKSTITCH (1 strand)

DMC	ANCHOR	COLORS
721	925	Medium orange spice
964	185	Light sea green
3801	1098	Very dark melon

FRENCH KNOT (3 strands, wrapped once)

DMC	ANCHOR	COLOR
310	403	Black

Letter placement

To personalize, use Petite Alphabet (page 11).
Model was stitched on beige 14-count Aida fabric from Charles Craft using DMC floss. Stitch desired name, then stitch icicles below and backstitch border around it. Name on sample was stitched with #498 dark red.

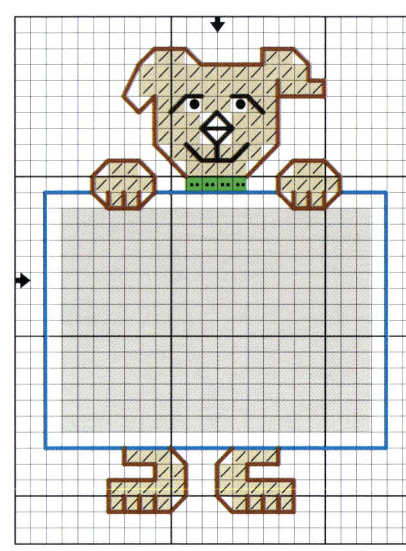

Puppy Frame

Design Size
22 wide x 29 high

CROSS-STITCH (2 strands)

DMC	ANCHOR	COLORS
701	227	Light green
3045	888	Dark yellow beige

BACKSTITCH (2 strands)

DMC	ANCHOR	COLORS
334	977	Medium baby blue
434	310	Light brown

BACKSTITCH (1 strand)

DMC	ANCHOR	COLOR
3371	382	Black brown

FRENCH KNOT (1 strand, wrapped twice)

DMC	ANCHOR	COLOR
3371	382	Black brown

Letter placement

To personalize, use Basic Bold Alphabet (page 14). Model shown on back cover was stitched on white 14-count Aida fabric with blue gingham trim infant bib from Charles Craft using DMC floss. Initial on sample was stitched with #350 medium coral.

Kitty Frame

Design Size
25 wide x 28 high

CROSS-STITCH (2 strands)

DMC	ANCHOR	COLOR
210	108	Medium lavender

BACKSTITCH (1 strand)

DMC	ANCHOR	COLORS
333	119	Very dark blue violet
3831	29	Dark raspberry

STRAIGHT STITCH (2 strands)

DMC	ANCHOR	COLORS
3326	36	Light rose (nose)
3831	29	Dark raspberry (collar)

FRENCH KNOT (3 strands, wrapped twice)

DMC	ANCHOR	COLOR
912	209	Light emerald green

ATTACH BEAD

● 3mm silver

Letter placement

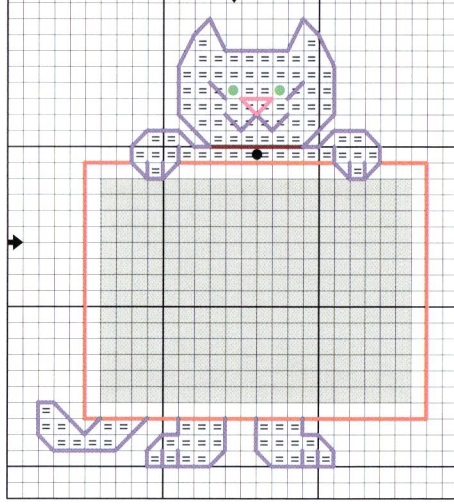

To personalize, use Basic Bold Alphabet (page 14). Model shown on back cover was stitched on white 14-count Aida fabric with pink gingham trim infant bib from Charles Craft using DMC floss and one silver bead. Initial on sample was stitched with #3326 light rose.

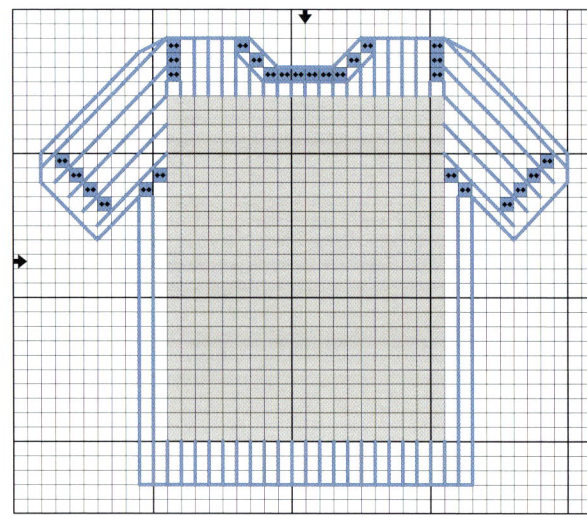

Team Shirt

Design Size
38 wide x 31 high

CROSS-STITCH (2 strands)

DMC	ANCHOR	COLOR
799	136	Medium delft blue

BACKSTITCH (2 strands)

DMC	ANCHOR	COLOR
799	136	Medium delft blue

Letter placement

To personalize, use Sportswear Alphabet (page 9). Model was stitched on white 14-count-Aida from Charles Craft using DMC floss. Work letter first, then work neckband and outline centered on letter. Fill in stripes with Backstitch last. Initial on sample was worked with #796 dark royal blue and #946 medium burnt orange with white backstitches.

6 • Personalize It With Cross-Stitch

American School of Needlework • Berne, Indiana 46711 • DRGnetwork.com

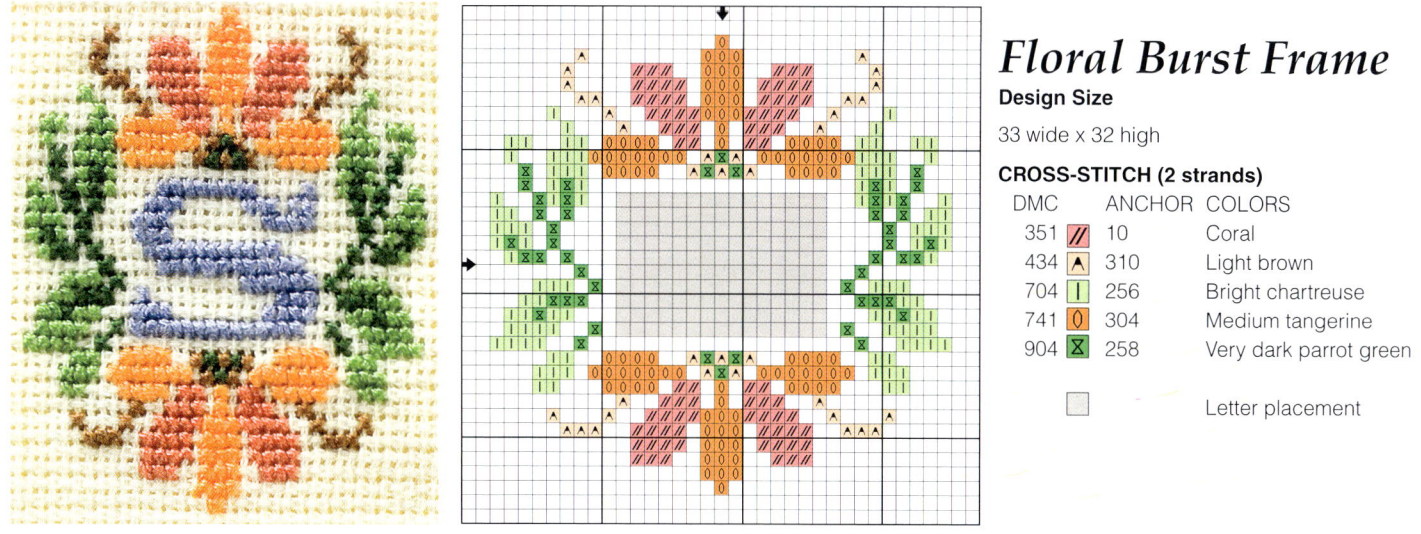

Floral Burst Frame

Design Size
33 wide x 32 high

CROSS-STITCH (2 strands)

DMC	ANCHOR	COLORS
351	10	Coral
434	310	Light brown
704	256	Bright chartreuse
741	304	Medium tangerine
904	258	Very dark parrot green
		Letter placement

To personalize, use Weekend Alphabet (below).
Model shown on back cover was stitched on ecru 11-count hand towel from Charles Craft using DMC floss. Initial on sample was stitched, omitting backstitches, with #3839 medium lavender blue.

Weekend Alphabet

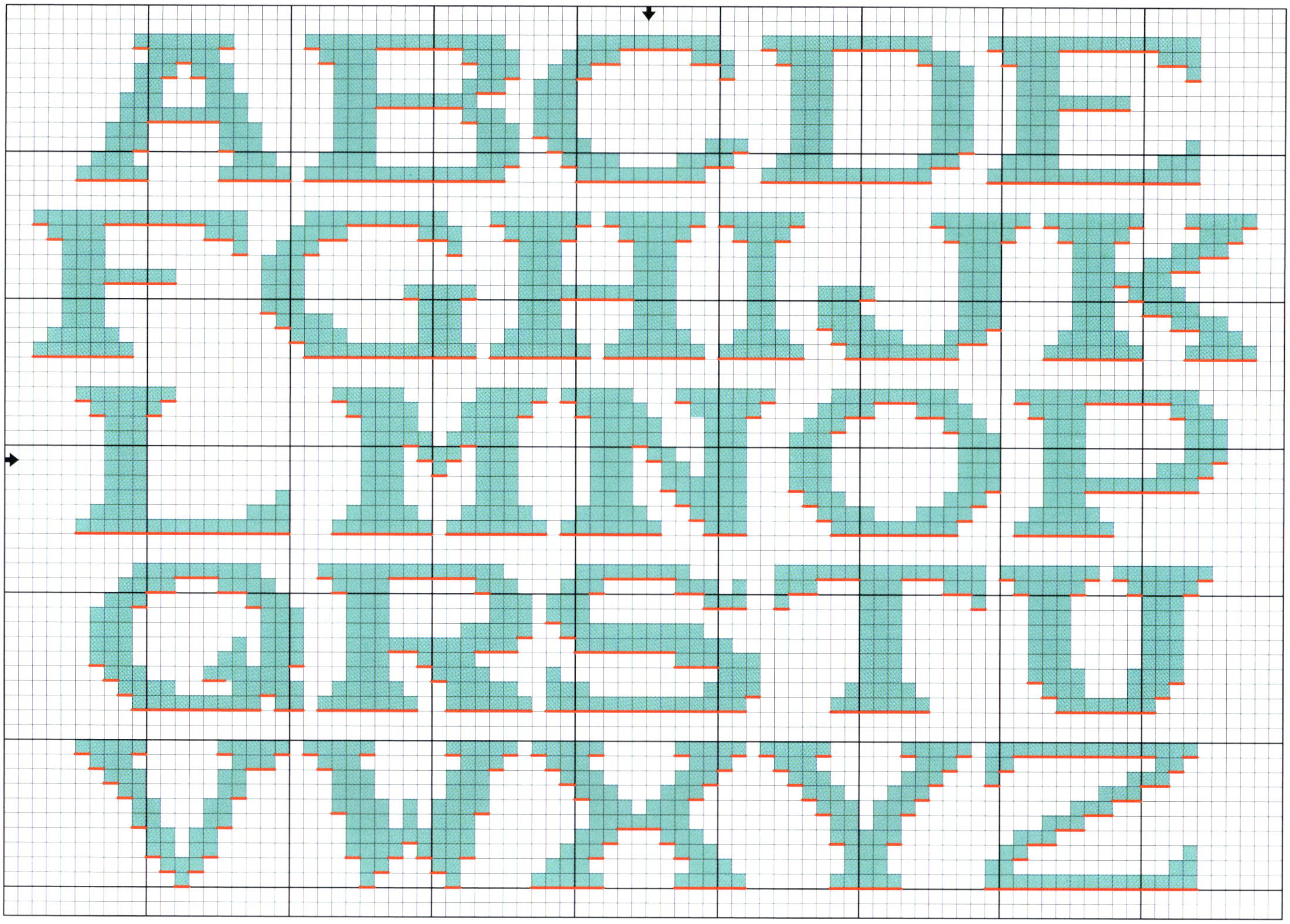

Semiformal Alphabet

Sportswear Alphabet

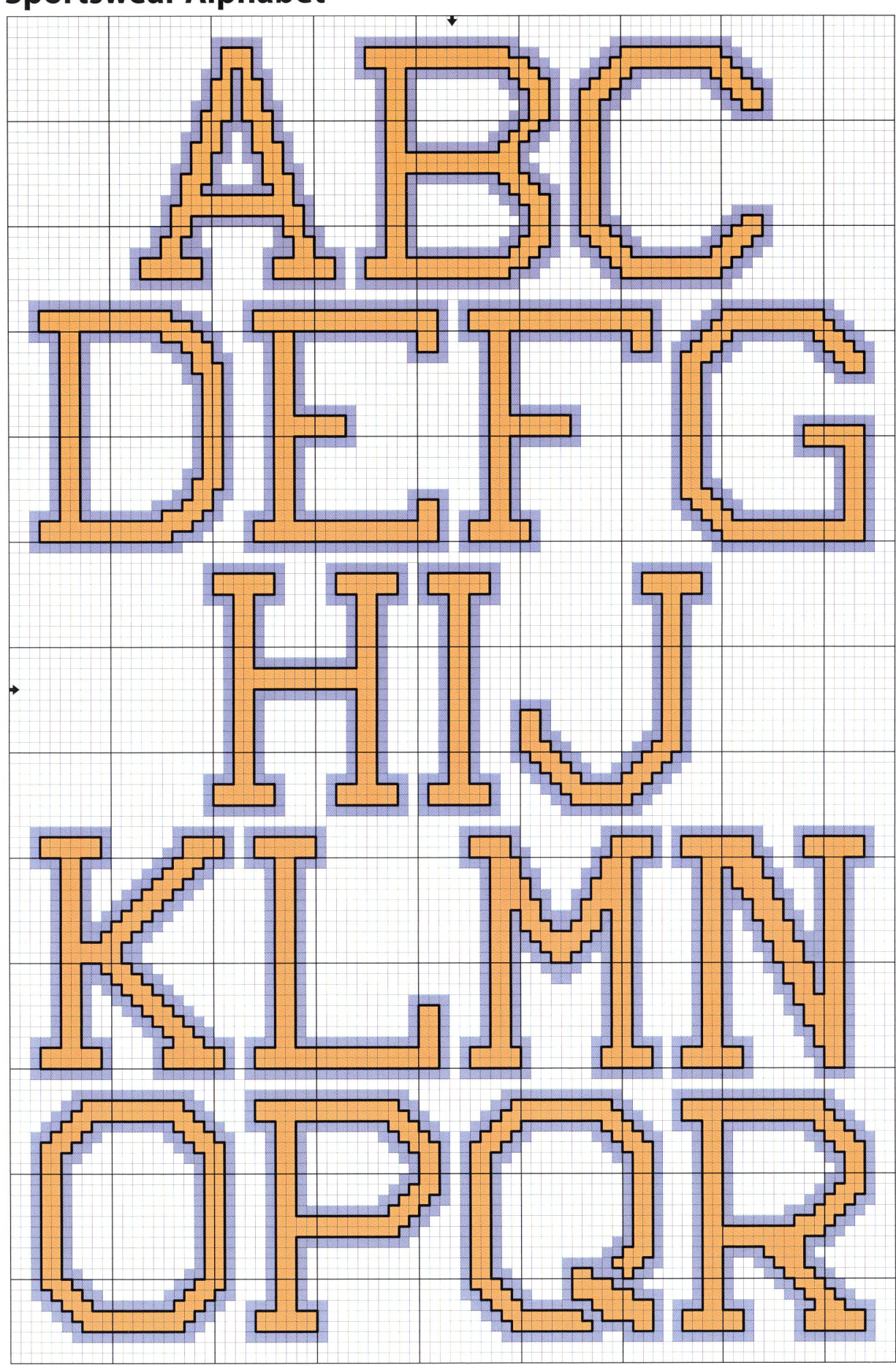

Country Casual Alphabet

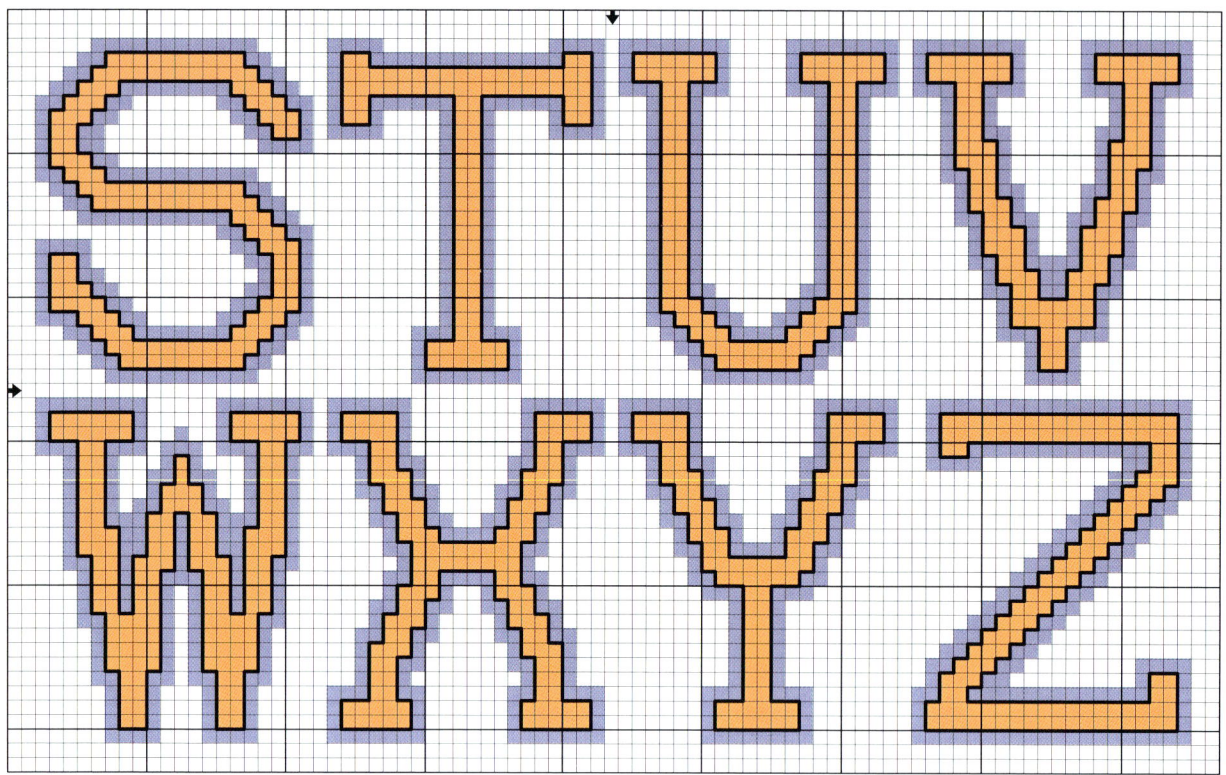

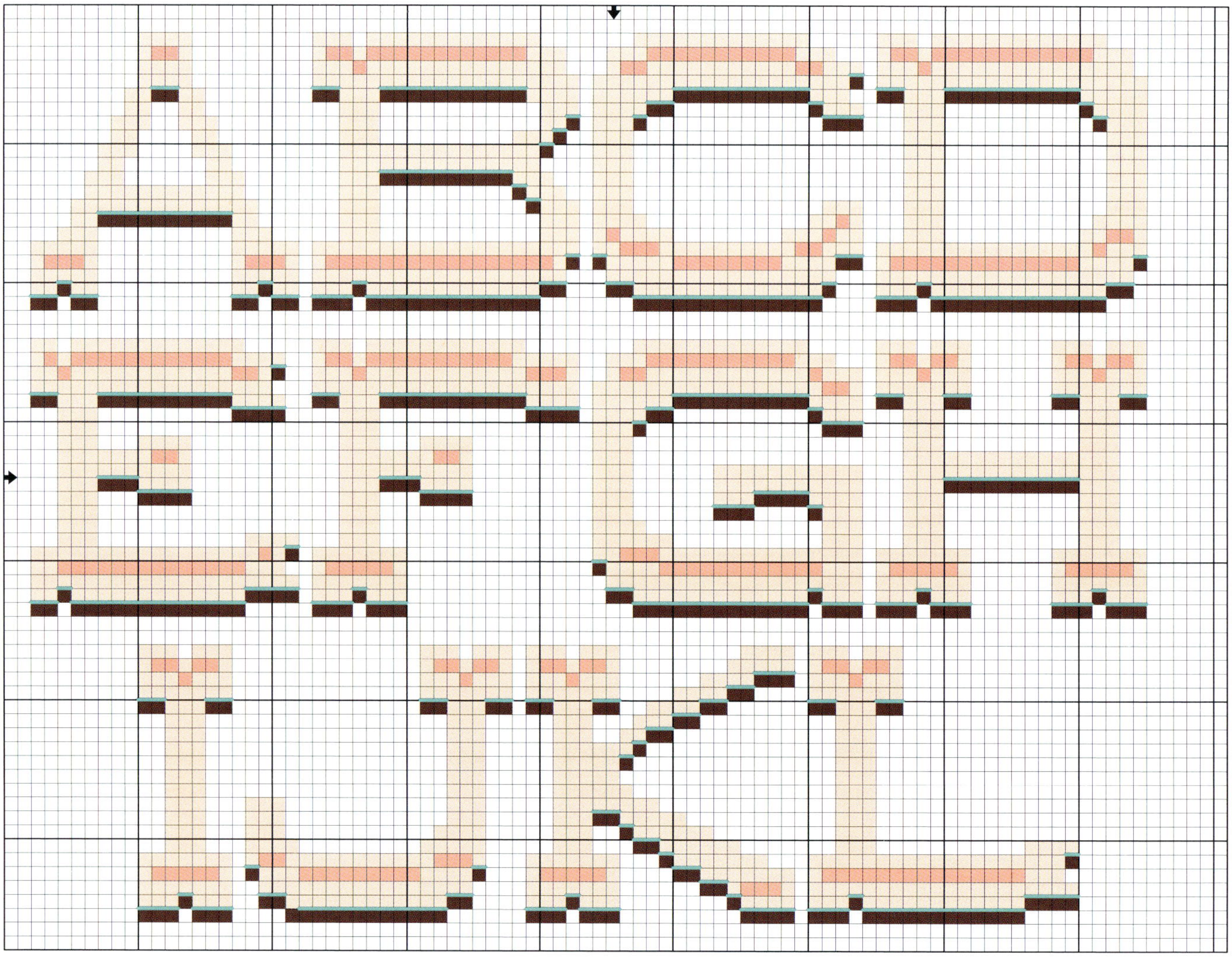

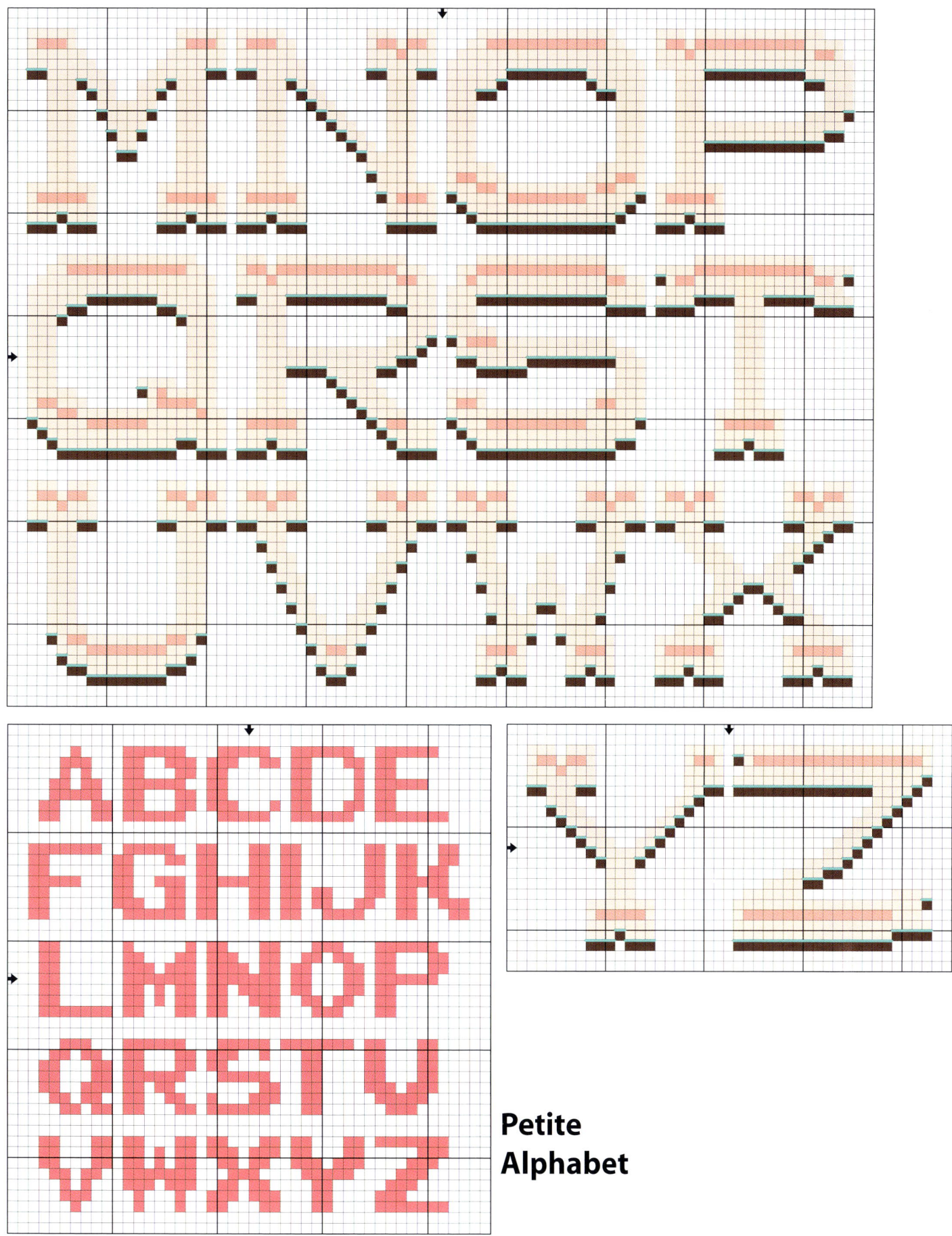

Petite Alphabet

Super Size Alphabet

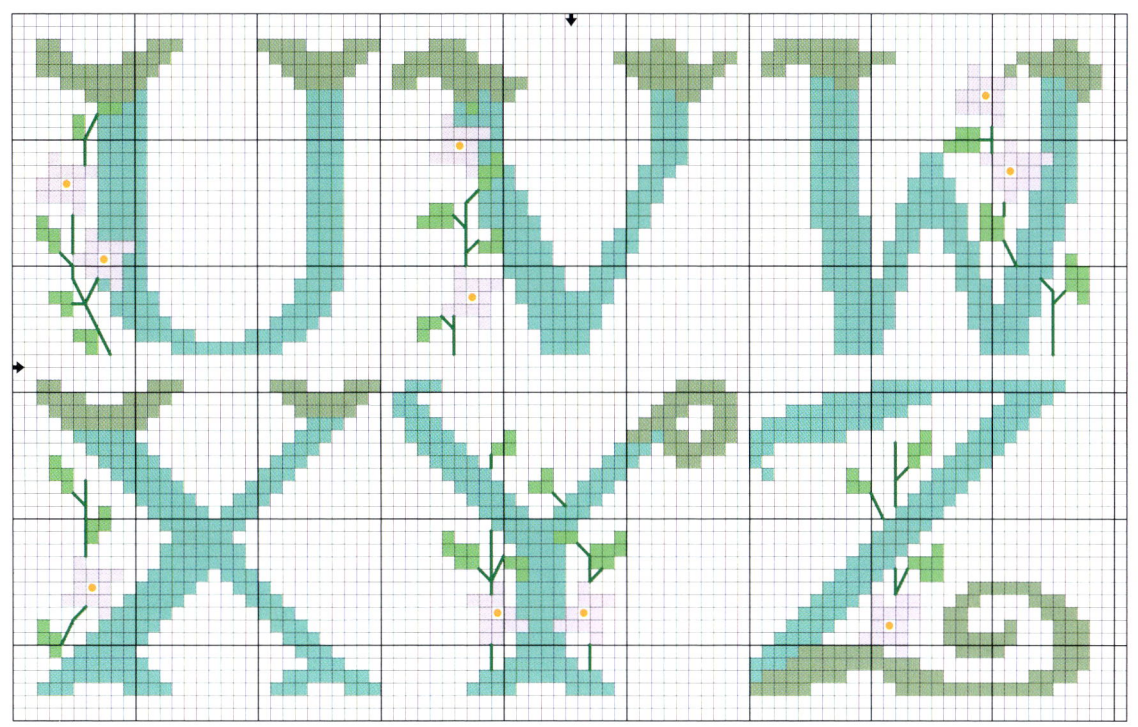

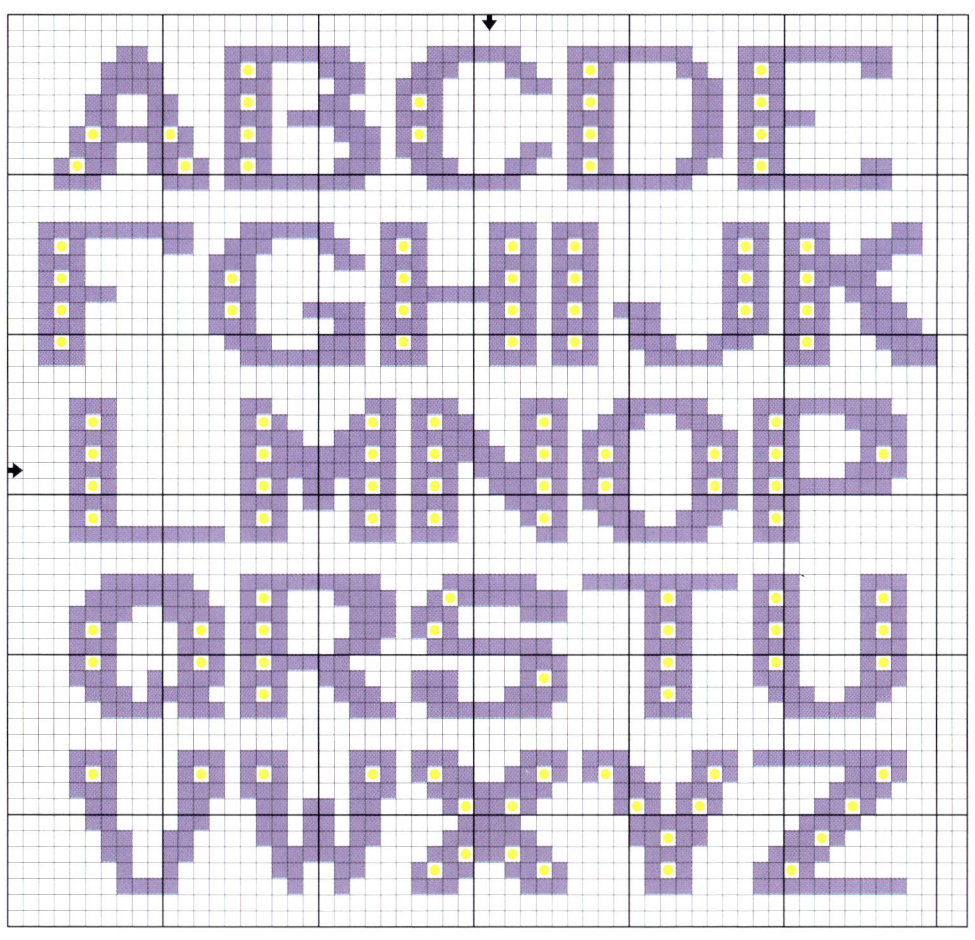

Junior Glamour Alphabet

ATTACH RHINESTONE
● 3mm crystal

Basic Bold Alphabet

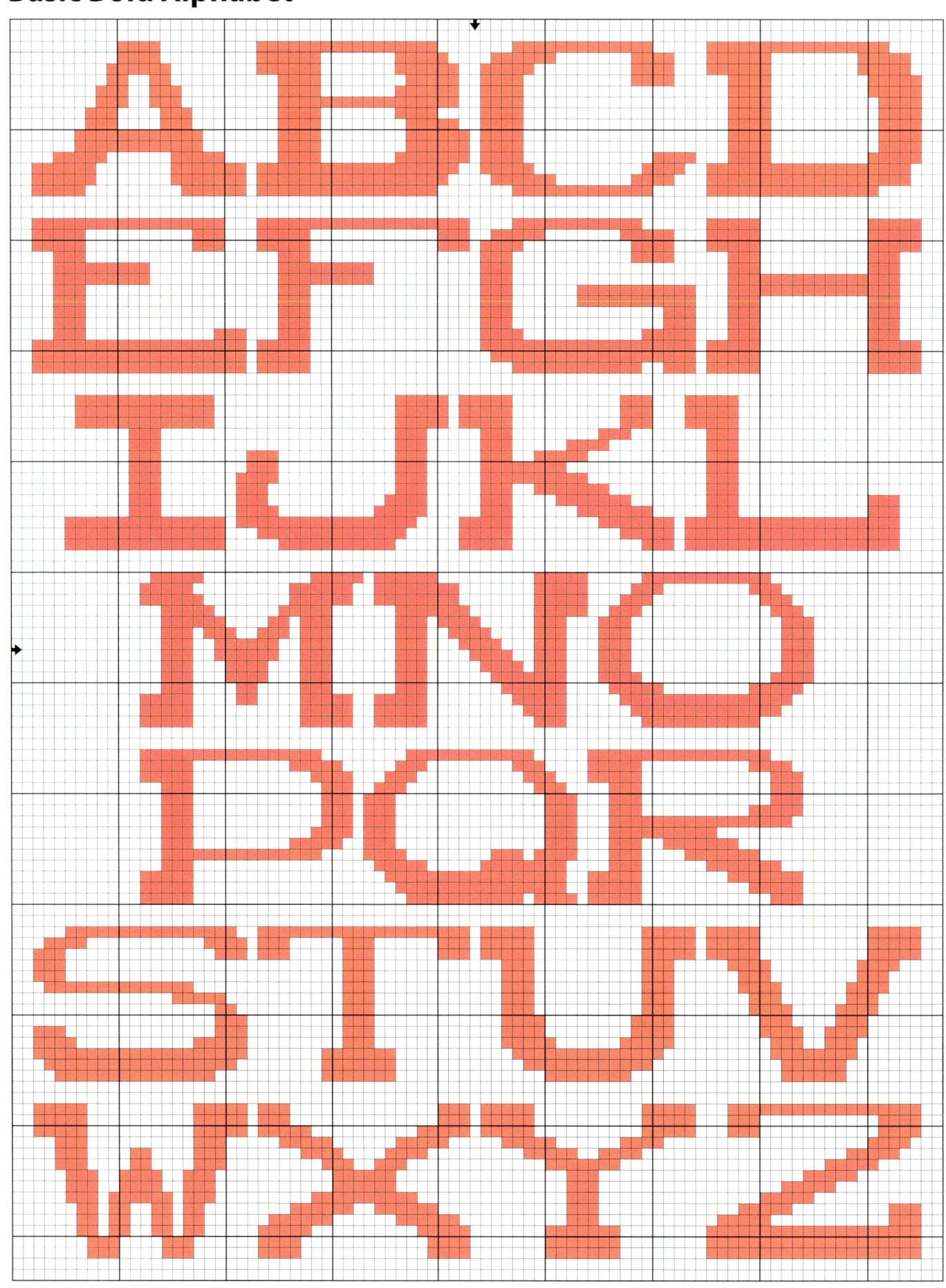

How to Stitch

WORKING FROM CHARTED DESIGNS

A square on a chart corresponds to a space for a Cross-Stitch on the stitching surface. The symbol in a square shows the floss color to be used for the stitch. The width and height for the design stitch-area are given; centers are shown by arrows. Backstitches, Straight Stitches and Running Stitches are shown by straight lines, and French Knots by dots.

FABRICS

Our cover models were worked on 11-count and 14-count Aida fabric. Aida cloth is an even-weave fabric that has the same number of horizontal and vertical threads (or blocks of threads) per inch. That number is called the thread count.

The size of the design is determined by the size of the even-weave fabric on which you work. Use the chart below as a guide to determine the finished size of a design on various popular sizes of Aida cloth.

Thread Count	Number of Stitches in Design				
	10	20	30	40	50
11-count	1"	1¾"	2¾"	3⅝"	4½"
14-count	¾"	1⅜"	2⅛"	2⅞"	3⅝"
16-count	⅝"	1¼"	1⅞"	2½"	3⅛"
18-count	½"	1⅛"	1⅝"	2¼"	2¾"

(measurements are given to the nearest ⅛")

NEEDLES

A blunt-tipped tapestry needle, size 24 or 26, is used for stitching on 14-count fabrics. The higher the needle number, the smaller the needle. The correct-size needle is easy to thread with the amount of floss required, but is not so large that it will distort the holes in the fabric. The following chart indicates the appropriate-size needle for each size of fabric, along with the suggested number of strands of floss to use.

Fabric	Stitches Per Inch	Strands of Floss	Tapestry Needle Size
Aida	11	3	22 or 24
Aida	14	2	24 or 26
Aida	16	2	24, 26 or 28
Aida	18	1 or 2	26 or 28

FLOSS

Our cover designs were stitched with DMC 6-strand embroidery floss. Anchor floss numbers are also listed. The companies have different color ranges, so these are only suggested substitutions. Floss color names are given. Cut floss into comfortable working lengths—we suggest about 18 inches. Use two strands of floss to Cross-Stitch on a 14-count fabric (as used for our cover stitching) unless otherwise noted in the color key. Use one strand of floss for Backstitches and French Knots unless otherwise noted.

GETTING STARTED

To begin in an unstitched area, bring threaded needle from back to front of fabric. Hold an inch of the end against the back, and then hold it in place with your first few stitches. To end threads and begin new ones next to existing stitches, weave through the backs of several stitches.

THE STITCHES

Use two strands of floss for all Cross-Stitches, and one strand for Backstitches, Straight Stitches, Running Stitches and French Knots, unless otherwise noted in the color key.

Cross-Stitch

The Cross-Stitch is formed in two motions. Follow the numbering in Fig. 1 and bring needle up at 1, down at 2, up at 3, down at 4, to complete the stitch. Work horizontal rows of stitches (Fig. 2) wherever possible. Bring thread up at 1, work half of each stitch across the row, and then complete the stitches on your return.

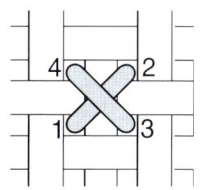

Fig. 1
Cross-Stitch

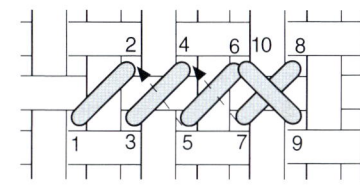

Fig. 2
Cross-Stitch Horizontal Row

Backstitch

Backstitches are worked after Cross-Stitches have been completed. They may slope in any direction and are occasionally worked over more than one square of fabric. Fig. 3 shows the progression of several stitches; bring thread up at odd numbers and down at even numbers. Frequently you must choose where to end one Backstitch color and begin the next color. Choose the object that should appear closest to you. Backstitch around that shape with the appropriate color, and then

Backstitch the areas behind it with adjacent color(s).

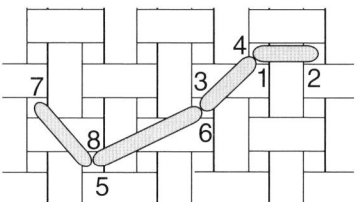

Fig. 3 Backstitch

French Knot

Bring thread up where indicated on chart. Wrap floss once around needle (Fig. 4) and reinsert needle at 2, close to 1, but at least one fabric thread away from it. Hold wrapping thread tightly and pull needle through, letting thread go just as knot is formed. For a larger knot, use more strands of floss.

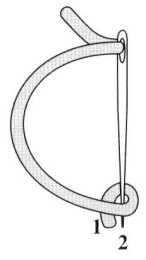

Fig. 4 French Knot

Lazy Daisy

This is a decorative stitch that is often worked on top of completed work. The chart will show the exact placement and length of each stitch (Fig. 5). Bring needle up at 1, make a loop, and go down into same hole. Bring needle up at 2 inside the loop and pull gently to adjust the size and shape of the loop. Go down at 3 to secure loop. Be sure to anchor end especially well on the wrong side.

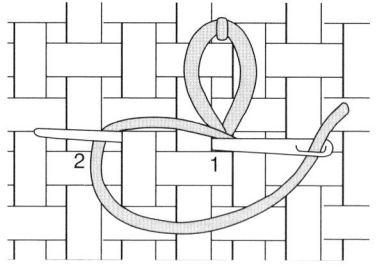

Fig. 5 Lazy Daisy

PLANNING A PROJECT

Choose the design you like and chart it on graph paper for exact planning. The spacing between letters is a matter of taste and depends on the effect you want to achieve.

When using frames, you will need to extend the frames border to the length you need. Each charted frame has information to guide you.

If you are working on a premade item, make sure there is a large enough stitching area available for your planned letters. If you are working on a piece of fabric, determine the stitched size; then allow enough additional fabric around the design plus 2 or 3 inches more on each side for use in finishing and mounting.

Cut your fabric exactly true, right along the holes of the fabric. Some raveling may occur as you handle the fabric. To minimize raveling along the raw edges use an overcast basting stitch, machine zigzag stitch, or masking tape, which you can cut away when you are finished.

FINISHING NEEDLEWORK

When you have finished stitching, dampen your embroidery (or, if soiled, wash in lukewarm mild soapsuds and rinse well). Roll in a towel to remove excess moisture. Place facedown on a dry towel or padded surface, and press carefully until dry and smooth. Make sure all thread ends are well anchored and clipped closely. Proceed with desired finishing. ∎

Copyright © 2008 DRG, 306 East Parr Road, Berne, IN 46711. All rights reserved.
This publication may not be reproduced in part or in whole without written permission from the publisher.

TOLL-FREE ORDER LINE or to request a free catalog (800) 582-6643
Customer Service (800) 282-6643, **Fax** (800) 882-6643
Visit DRGnetwork.com.

We have made every effort to ensure the accuracy and completeness of these instructions.
We cannot, however, be responsible for human error, typographical mistakes or variations in individual work.

ISBN: 978-1-59012-213-6   All rights reserved.   Printed in USA   1 2 3 4 5 6 7 8 9